S0-AXO-526

Gordon Gregory Middle School
2621 Springdale Circle
Naperville, IL 60564

S0-AXO-526

OUR WORLD
OUR FUTURE

Protecting Forests

Sharon Dalgleish

CHELSEA HOUSE
PUBLISHERS
A Haights Cross Communications Company
Philadelphia

This edition first published in 2003 in the United States of America by Chelsea House Publishers, a subsidiary of Haights Cross Communications.

Chelsea House Publishers
1974 Sproul Road, Suite 400
Broomall, PA 19008-0914

The Chelsea House world wide web address is www.chelseahouse.com

Library of Congress Cataloging-in-Publication Data Applied for.
ISBN 0-7910-7017-4

First published in 2002 by
MACMILLAN EDUCATION AUSTRALIA PTY LTD
627 Chapel Street, South Yarra, Australia, 3141

Copyright © Sharon Dalgleish 2002
Copyright in photographs © individual photographers as credited

Edited by Sally Woollett
Text design by Karen Young
Cover design by Karen Young
Page layout and simple diagrams by Nina Sanadze
Technical illustrations and maps by Pat Kermode, Purple Rabbit Productions

Printed in China

Acknowledgements
Cover photograph: Tasmanian rainforest, courtesy of Geoff Murray/Tasmanian Photo Library.

AFP Photo/Robyn Beck/Newspix, p. 13 (bottom); ANT Photo Library, p. 11 (bottom); Keith Kent—Peter Arnold/Auscape, p. 11 (top); Edward Parker—OSF/Auscape, p. 7 (center right); Australian Picture Library/Corbis, pp. 7 (far right), 15 (top), 17 (left), 25 (bottom); Coo-ee Picture Library, pp. 14 (top left), 20 (top); The DW Stock Picture Library, pp. 4 (top left, top center, top right and bottom left), 6 (top), 7 (center left), 12 (top), 14 (bottom left), 23 (top); Victor Englebert, pp. 6 (bottom), 9, 12 (bottom), 13 (top), 14 (right), 16 (right), 17 (right), 18, 23 (bottom), 24 (right), 25 (top); Forest Stewardship Council, p. 28; Getty Images/Photodisc, pp. 4 (bottom center), 19, 20 (bottom), 30; Getty Images/Tony Stone, p. 16 (left); Imageaddict.com, p. 4 (bottom right); © 2001 Mark A. Johnson, p. 21 (top); Fred Adler/Kino Archives, p. 8; Dennis Sarson/Lochman Transparencies, pp. 10, 21 (bottom); © R. Berriedale-Johnson/Panos Pictures, p. 24 (left); Brian Parker, pp. 14 (center left), 15 (bottom); Southern Images/Silkstone, p. 7 (far left); Mark Edwards/Still Pictures, p. 29.

While every care has been taken to trace and acknowledge copyright, the publisher tenders their apologies for any accidental infringement where copyright has proved untraceable.

Contents

READ
MORE ABOUT:

Look out for this box. It will tell you the other pages in this book where you can find out more about related topics.

Our world

We are connected to everything in our world. We are connected through the air we breathe, the water we drink, the food we eat, the energy we use, and the soil we live on.

To keep our world healthy, all these elements must work together.

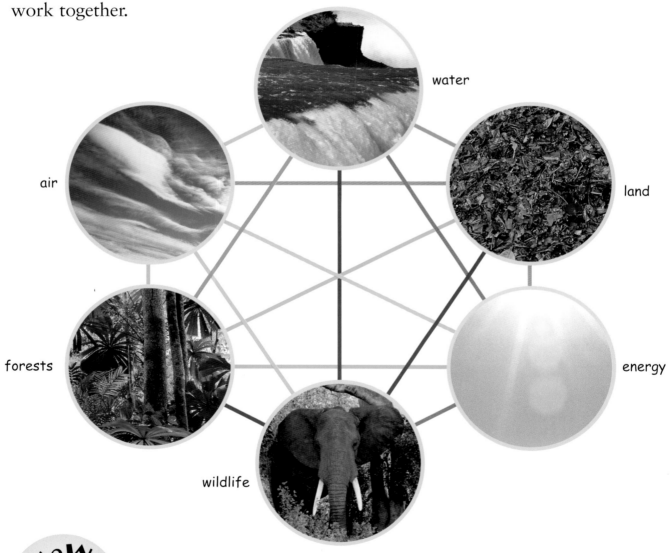

water

land

energy

wildlife

forests

air

SHOW ME The parts of your body work together to keep you healthy. If one part of your body stops working properly, you get sick!

Our future

The number of people in our world is now doubling every 40 years. This means that when you are grown up there could be twice as many people on Earth as there are now.

Every person on Earth needs certain things to survive. We need to make sure our world will still be able to give people everything they need to live, now and in the future.

▲ Now.

▲ Forty years from now.

STOP & THINK

Suppose that one part of our world were to stop working properly. What do you think might happen to the rest of our world?

5

Forest facts

About a quarter of the land surface of our world is covered with forests. A forest is a large area of land covered with trees. There are thousands of different **species** of trees, but they do not all grow in the same forest. The type of tree that grows in a forest depends on the type of weather.

Boreal forests grow in the northern regions of Europe, Asia and North America. These parts of the world have long, cold winters and short summers. The trees are cone shaped so the snow can slide right off without breaking the branches.

Temperate forests grow in areas where the weather is milder. The summers are warm and the winters cool. Some temperate forests have evergreen trees, which keep their leaves all year round. In areas with colder winters, most of the trees are deciduous. This means they shed their leaves in autumn and grow new ones in spring.

Tropical forests grow in areas close to the **equator**. This is the hottest part of the world, where there is warm, wet weather all year round. Tropical rainforests have many types of trees growing closely together.

▲ Forests grow in every part of our world except in the Arctic and Antarctic, where it is too cold, and in sandy deserts, where it is too dry. ▼

SHOW ME — Where do you live? Find your country on a map of the world. Do you live in a warm place close to the equator or in a cold place far from the equator? What type of forest grows in your region?

6

Covered in trees

There are thousands of different species of trees in our world, all with different ways of surviving the **climate** where they grow.

TYPES OF FORESTS

Forest type	boreal	temperate deciduous	temperate evergreen	tropical
Trees that grow there	fir, spruce, pine	beech, birch, maple, oak, poplar	redwood, sequoia, cedar, pine	mahogany, teak

About 8,000 years ago our world was covered in about 15 billion acres (6 billion hectares) of forests.

STOP & THINK
What happens when we cut the trees down?

7

Green clean-air machines

There is one thing all green trees and plants have in common. They all take in **carbon dioxide** and let out **oxygen**, which is just as well for people and animals. We breathe in oxygen and breathe out carbon dioxide. It is a balanced cycle.

Today, forests cover only half the area they did 8,000 years ago. Of this surviving forest, just more than 2.5 billion acres (1 billion hectares) is surviving native forest that has not been disturbed in some way by people. That means we have lost nearly 80 percent of the original forests that once covered our world!

Original forest

Forest today

Old-growth forest today

5 10 15

Forest area (billion acres)

▲ We have lost most of the forests that were originally on Earth.

▶ Next time you get a chance, stand under a tree and look up. Try to count how many leaves the tree has. Can you imagine how much area all those leaves would take up if you were to lay them all side by side? Each of those leaves is taking in the carbon dioxide that we breathe out.

STOP & THINK
What will happen if there are fewer trees in the future?

Disturbing the balance

Many of our original forests have been lost. This is because we are cutting down trees for timber, to make paper, and to clear ground for towns and farms.

Fewer trees in the world means fewer clean-air machines to use up the carbon dioxide and to produce oxygen. This means that the natural balance between the amounts of carbon dioxide and oxygen has been disturbed.

◄ The rainforests in Brazil have been called the lungs of the world. They help control the amount of carbon dioxide in the **atmosphere**.

SHOW ME

Every 20 seconds 2.5 acres (1 hectare) of rainforest in Brazil is cut down. That is about a football field every two seconds. How long did it take you to read this page? How many football fields of rainforest have just been lost?

READ MORE ABOUT:

• clearing the forests for cities and farms on page 12
• logging forests for timber on page 18.

OUR WORLD

Green forest or greenhouse?

The carbon dioxide in our world's atmosphere acts like a sheet of glass on a greenhouse. It lets the sunlight through but does not let all the heat back out—just like inside a real greenhouse. This greenhouse effect keeps Earth warmer than it would otherwise be. Without it our world would be covered in ice.

Coal, oil and gas are really carbon stores of energy from the sun. Over millions of years the dead remains of animals and plants have been pressed deep underground and turned into coal, oil and gas. Coal, oil and gas are called fossil fuels. When we burn these fuels in cars, factories and power stations, the stored carbon is released into the atmosphere as carbon dioxide. When there is too much carbon dioxide in our atmosphere, and too few trees to use it up, the greenhouse effect becomes a problem.

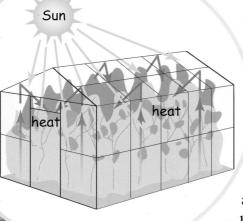

▲ Greenhouses are used mainly in cold countries. The heat trapped inside helps the flowers and vegetables grow.

STOP & THINK

What will happen if there is too much carbon dioxide in the atmosphere?

▲ Nearly one-quarter of the carbon dioxide in our world's atmosphere comes from burning forests. When forests are cut down, smaller trees, shrubs and branches are often burned. Not only do we lose the clean-air machines, but the burning process releases even more carbon dioxide!

10

Storm warning!

When there is too much carbon dioxide in the atmosphere, it traps too much heat. Then our world gets even warmer. This warmer weather—called **global warming**—does not mean more sunshine. Scientists think it will change the weather patterns in our world. This means there will be more floods, storms, droughts, hurricanes and other unusual weather. Plants and animals will die because they will not be able to live in the new weather conditions.

In some places people are planting trees to grow new forests. A growing tree takes in more carbon dioxide than a tree that is already fully grown. That is good news for our world.

▲ Changing weather patterns mean more unusual weather.

◄ The mountain forest home of the Siberian tiger is getting warmer and wetter.

YOU CAN DO IT!

◆ Plant a tree. Trees take in carbon dioxide and give out clean oxygen for us to breathe.

◆ Most electricity is made by burning fossil fuels, which release carbon dioxide. So save as much electricity as you can. Here are some ways you can do it:

◆ Turn lights off when you leave the room.

◆ Ask your parents to buy energy-saving lightbulbs.

◆ Turn the heat down. If you are cold, put on more clothes.

◆ Use air conditioners and fans as little as possible. If you are hot, make a fan out of recycled paper.

READ
MORE ABOUT:

- carbon dioxide on page 8
- replanting trees on page 19.

Making space

The number of people living in our world is growing by 90 million people a year. More than half of all the people in our world live in cities. These cities cover twice as much land today as they did 20 years ago. Land that was once covered in forests is now paved in concrete.

Because there are more people in our world, we need to grow more food to feed them. Forests are also cut down to make room for more farmland. Instead of trees, crops are grown in the soil.

▲ In many parts of our world, concrete jungles have replaced living, breathing forests.

▲ Huge areas of forest have been cleared for farming. Most of this forest in Brazil has been burned to make room for cattle.

STOP & THINK
What happens to the land when the trees are gone?

12

Losing more than trees

Trees do more than clean the air we breathe. Large tree roots hold the soil in place. A blanket of fallen leaves protects the soil and holds it in place. Without trees, the soil can easily be swept away by wind and rain. This process is called soil erosion.

Chopping down trees can cause floods, too. Forests hold and use large amounts of water. They are a bit like giant sponges! But when forests are cleared, the water can run straight off the land, into rivers and out to sea.

Some countries have organized replanting programs to stop floods from destroying their towns.

▲ You can see where the level of the land used to be before all the trees were cut down.

How forests help to stop floods

- Some rainwater stays on leaves and **evaporates**.
- Leaves make the rain fall more gently on the ground, causing less erosion.
- Tree roots absorb water. The dry soil can then store more rainwater.

▲ When the Yangtze River flooded in 1998, the Chinese government tried to blame it all on heavy rain. But the area had lost 85 percent of its forest cover in just 20 years. There is now a plan to replant the area.

YOU CAN DO IT!

- If you live on a farm, plant a row of trees beside each field. The trees' roots will hold on to the soil so that it does not blow away.
- Eat less meat, especially beef. Beef often comes from cattle that were raised on land cleared in rainforests.
- Plant trees near your school.

READ MORE ABOUT:

- floods on page 17.

Digging under

▲ Ceramic mugs are made from clay (a soft rock).

▲ The plastic in this stereo comes from oil or coal, and electricity to play it is generated from coal.

▲ Car bodies are made of steel, which is produced from iron ore.

Since 1950, people in **developed countries** have **consumed** as much as all the people from the past added together. The big growth in the number of people living in our world has meant a big growth in the demand for raw materials. **Developing countries** once used only a small amount of raw materials. Now they are using more.

Some of the **raw materials** we use to make many of the things we buy come from trees. Other raw materials come from the rocks that lie beneath the trees. To get the raw materials that are buried in the ground, we have to dig them out of a quarry or mine. But to make the quarry or mine we have to first clear the trees. As a mine or quarry grows, it creates huge piles of waste. Then more land has to be cleared to store that waste.

▲ Mining companies also build roads through forests. This road in the Amazon rainforest in Brazil allows more people through. This will disturb the natural forest even more.

STOP & THINK
Raw materials can be made into all kinds of useful and fun things, but do we always need to buy so much?

Reclaim the land

Land can be ruined by careless mining. Nothing can live there, and the scar will remain for hundreds of years.

If we use **resources** more carefully, then we will not have to dig as many mines to supply them. Some mines that already exist, but are not used anymore, can be cleaned up and planted with grass or trees. Some countries have strict rules that a mine site must be put back to its natural state after mining is finished. This costs a lot of money, and it is not always possible to make the poisonous waste from the mining process safe again.

▲ This iron ore mine in Brazil was once covered in rainforest.

◀ Part of this tin mine in Thailand has been reclaimed as a holiday resort.

YOU CAN DO IT!

- Before you buy something, think about where the raw materials to make it came from. Is it worth it? Do you really need to buy it? Only buy it if the answer is "yes."

- Try not to buy things that are meant to be thrown away, such as disposable cameras or paper plates. Buy high-quality products and keep them for a lifetime. You will not need to keep going back to buy more—and we will not need to clear so many forests to reach the raw materials below.

- Do not buy silly, useless things just because they are there. If you stop buying them, raw materials and forests will not be used to make them.

Water on tap

You are feeling thirsty so you go into the kitchen and turn on the faucet. Easy! But did you ever stop and wonder how the water got into the faucet? Much of the water we use comes from lakes. Where there are no natural lakes, people often make one by building a dam across a river. In rainy weather the water collects behind a dam and is stored in a **reservoir**. Dams are built to supply the huge amounts of water used in factories and homes every day.

In addition to using a lot of water, we are changing the amount of rain that falls by cutting down rainforests. As water evaporates from the rainforests, clouds form. These clouds carry rain to other places. Without the rainforests, this rain is no longer made, so we need the water from dams even more.

▲ A dam controls the flow of water down a river.

▶ Cutting down rainforests changes the amount of rain that falls.

STOP & THINK
What happens to the land around a river when a reservoir is made?

16

Drowning trees

When a reservoir is created, huge areas of land are flooded. Thousands of square miles of rainforest have been lost in this way. When the rainforest is destroyed, all the living things that lived there have to find somewhere else to live.

▲ Can you see trees sticking out of the water in this picture? This land used to be covered in forest.

◀ Dams have been built in the Amazon rainforest to create **hydroelectricity**. The Itaipu dam in Brazil flooded a huge area of rainforest.

YOU CAN DO IT!

- Use less water at home. Then we will not need to store so much water in reservoirs.

- Take short showers, and turn off the faucet while you brush your teeth.

- Put a container outside to catch rainwater. Use it to water plants instead of using water from the faucet.

17

Mountains of wood

We use wood every day. In some parts of the world, especially in developing countries, wood is the main fuel used for cooking and heating. We also use wood to build houses and furniture. We use up whole forests of trees to make paper products such as phone books, tissues, toilet paper, paper plates and office paper.

What is wood used for?

- 50 percent for fuel
- 33 percent for building
- 17 percent for paper

A city newspaper can use as many as 500,000 trees to print one day's edition.

▲ Pine trees are cut into mountains of tiny wood chips to be used to make paper.

Using more paper

- In 1950 the average person in our world used 31 pounds (14 kilograms) of paper in a year.
- In 1960 they used 55 pounds (25 kilograms) of paper.
- By 1997 the average person was using 110 pounds (50 kilograms) of paper.

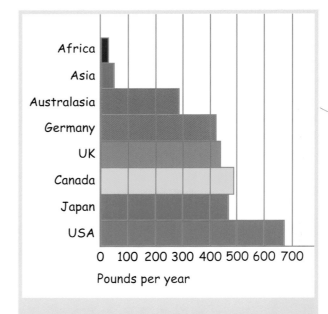

▲ Some countries use much more paper than others. This graph shows how much paper per person was used around our world in 1999.

STOP & THINK
How can we make sure forest resources do not run out?

18

New forest for old

A big part of the problem today is that in the past, logged forests were not replanted. The supply of trees seemed endless. Today we know better. Many forests are managed so that new trees are planted to replace those that were cut down. Even so, trees are still being chopped down seven times faster than they are being planted.

When replanting happens, the trees are planted close together so they grow straight and with fewer branches. This makes timber that is easier to log. But it makes forests that do not have much room for other plants and animals to live. The good news is that by growing these **plantation forests** we should be able to produce wood without having to harm any more old-growth forests.

▲ These new forests have less variety of plants and animals than old-growth forests.

YOU CAN DO IT!

- Use less paper. Do not print out everything you do on the computer, only the things you really need.
- Recycle all the paper you use, and try to buy paper with a high recycled content.
- Ask your teacher if you can organize paper recycling at your school.
- Ask your parents if you can put a sign on your mailbox saying you do not want junk mail.
- Use cloth napkins and towels, not paper, so you can reuse them.

READ MORE ABOUT:

- old-growth forests on page 8
- plant and animal variety on page 22.

19

Acid and aliens

When fossil fuels are burned, they give off a mixture of polluting gases. When some of these gases mix with the water in clouds, they make **acid**. Then, instead of raining water, it rains acid!

There are different kinds of acids. Some, such as lemon juice, are weak. Acid rain is strong. It can burn holes in your clothes.

◀ In 1950 there were 50 million cars and trucks in our world. Today there are 500 million. One hundred thousand new cars are made every day. Each of them produces the gases that make acid rain.

◀ The pollution coming out of this factory smokestack is being released into the air.

STOP & THINK
What happens if acid rain falls in a forest?

20

Sick forests

Acid rain can kill fish in lakes and rivers. It can kill whole forests.

Pollution is not the only thing making forests sick. When a species of plant or animal is introduced to a place it has not lived in before, it is called an alien, exotic or introduced species. Alien species can reproduce and take over the whole area unchecked. They can also bring diseases with them.

▶ Logging equipment can bring disease into a forest. A fungus brought in on logging equipment killed thousands of jarrah trees, like the ones shown here, in Australia.

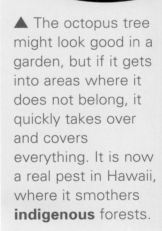

▲ The octopus tree might look good in a garden, but if it gets into areas where it does not belong, it quickly takes over and covers everything. It is now a real pest in Hawaii, where it smothers **indigenous** forests.

YOU CAN DO IT!

- Power stations produce pollution that makes acid rain, so do not waste electricity.
- Cars produce pollution that makes acid rain, so use your feet instead of the car.
- Factories produce pollution that makes acid rain, so reduce, reuse and recycle instead of always buying something new.
- If you have a garden, persuade your parents to plant species indigenous to your local area. That way alien seeds will not spread into indigenous forests.

READ MORE ABOUT:

- fossil fuels on page 10.

Rich world or poor world?

Tropical rainforests are home to the greatest variety of plants and animals in our world. There are five times as many tree species on the island of Madagascar than in the whole of North America. Hot, wet rainforests cover only 6 percent of our world's surface. Yet they are home to nearly 70 percent of our world's wildlife. This rich variety of wildlife is called **biodiversity**.

Some logging companies claim that forested land in developing countries is increasing because they are replanting trees as they clear the forests. This is true, but the plantation forests they are planting are replacing natural forests that had many different plants. The biodiversity has been lost.

The tallest, oldest trees in the forest break through the canopy. This emergent layer is home to more birds, animals and lizards.

The tree branches form a roof over the forest. This is the canopy. It is crowded with birds, mammals, snakes and frogs feeding on the leaves, seeds, flowers and fruits.

The understorey is dark, gloomy and humid. Here ferns, palms and vines drip with moisture, and lizards, fruit bats and spiders search for food.

The forest floor is dark and damp. Small animals, insects, fungi and bacteria live here.

▲ A tropical rainforest has a rich biodiversity because it has different **habitats**.

STOP & THINK
Are natural forests more valuable than plantation forests?

New discoveries

Plantation forests and non-natural forests are important. Their growing trees absorb large amounts of carbon dioxide to help reduce global warming. They also supply us with **renewable** timber. We can cut down the trees, use the timber as a raw material and then grow more trees in their place.

There is, however, a world of difference between these plantation forests and natural forests. Many of the foods we eat came originally from rainforests. Rainforest plants are also used to make medicine to treat some kinds of illnesses.

Each year hundreds of new plants are discovered, hidden in the rich growth of natural forests. These new plants could be useful, too. If we do not act to save the rainforests, we could lose many foods and medicinal plants before we even know their value.

▲ The rosy periwinkle plant grows in the rainforests in Madagascar. It is used to make a medicine to treat leukemia, a type of cancer.

◄ Brazil is one of the few countries left in our world with large areas of original natural forest. Yet huge areas of the Amazon rainforest are burned to clear the land for cattle farming, mining or roads. If we do not value natural forests above plantation forests, natural forests will be lost at an even faster rate.

YOU CAN DO IT!

● Reuse paper whenever you can. Be sure to write on both sides. Then recycle the paper when you are finished.

● Tell your parents not to buy furniture or other goods made from rainforest timber such as mahogany or teak. Use plantation timber or second-hand timber instead.

READ MORE ABOUT:

• managing forests on page 19.

23

OUR WORLD

Forest spirits

Trees and forests have different values to different people. Indigenous people around our world believe that forests are alive with spirit. Yanomami people living in the Amazon rainforest feel they belong to the forest. They say it is like a mother. It guides them and feeds them. Big businesses far away from the forests sometimes see the forest only as a supply of raw materials.

When people see the same thing in different ways, it can lead to arguments. A famous argument happened in a village in India in 1973. A sporting goods factory planned to log the forest that the villagers lived in and depended upon. The women hugged the trees, calling out "Chipko! Chipko!" In their language, *chipko* meant "to hug." The loggers could not chop down the trees without harming the people. Finally the government agreed to stop the logging.

▲ The Chipko movement began in India.

STOP & THINK
Do people have the right to destroy forests for their own needs?

► An oil company left this mess in the Amazon rainforest in Ecuador.

24

Protecting the future

Indigenous people have an important role to play in the future of natural forests. There are about 50 million indigenous people living in tropical rainforests. These people have a deep understanding of the forest and its wildlife. They know how to use the forest without destroying it. We need to value their rights to live in the rainforest. If everyone shares their skills and knowledge, we can all benefit from the rainforest and leave enough for the future.

▶ Some Hindu people hold ceremonies where they offer gifts to trees.

▲ In the Amazon rainforest, scientists are working with indigenous people to list all of the plants that indigenous people use for food and medicines. These scientists study the traditional plant medicines. They find the chemical ingredient in the plant and copy it to make drugs. One rainforest might hold cures for thousands of diseases.

YOU CAN DO IT!

- Get out into nature whenever you have the chance. See how amazing trees are—even if they are only in your own backyard.

- Try and visit a national park or reserve. Find out if there is anything you can do to help look after it.

- Support the rights of indigenous people to control their own land.

READ MORE ABOUT:

- rainforest food and medicine on page 23.

25

Tree journal

Sometimes we are so used to seeing trees around us that we do not even notice them anymore. Here is an activity to help you take notice—and find out how they grow and change.

What you need:

- notebook, pencils and crayons
- string
- measuring tape
- scissors
- plastic bags
- tape.

This project will take a whole year, so be sure to choose a tree that is easy and safe to visit.

What to do:

1 Take a walk near where you live, select a tree and draw it in your notebook.

2 Write down words to describe your tree. Does it have any unusual markings or patterns?

3 Tie a piece of string around the trunk, 36 inches (90 centimeters) from the ground. Cut the string and then measure it. This will give you the distance around the outside of the tree. Write it down.

4 Place a page from your notebook against the bark and rub a crayon over the paper.

5 Collect some fallen leaves in small plastic bags. Tape the bags inside the notebook.

6 Draw any birds, lizards, insects or other wildlife you see in or around the tree.

7 Visit your tree as often as you can and make entries in your journal for the next 12 months.

What happens?

You will notice many changes during the year that you have never seen or thought of before.

Make your own paper and help save a forest

Once you get used to making your own paper, you can make it even more special by adding interesting things to the paper mash in step 4. Try adding leaves or petals.

What you need:

- 1 adult helper
- scrap paper
- bowl
- 4 strips of wood
- fine wire mesh or screen
- hammer
- nails
- blotting paper
- newspaper
- potato masher
- rolling pin
- iron.

What to do:

1. Tear up the scrap paper and put it in the bowl. Ask the adult helper to pour on hot water. Leave it soaking while you make the screen in the next step.

2. Ask the adult helper to nail the four pieces of wood together to make a frame. Cover the frame with the fine wire mesh. Nail the mesh in place.

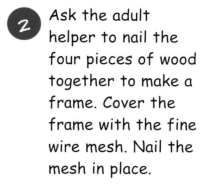

wire mesh

wooden frame

nails

3. Put some blotting paper on top of a few layers of newspaper.

4. When the soaking paper is really soft and mushy, mash it up with the potato masher.

5. Carefully pour some of the paper mash onto the screen. Let the water drain through.

6. Quickly flip the screen upside-down onto the blotting paper. Put another piece of blotting paper on top.

7. Roll the rolling pin over the top blotting paper. Squeeze out as much water as you can.

8. Ask your adult helper to iron the blotting paper until the recycled paper is almost dry.

9. Peel off the top blotting paper and leave the recycled paper to dry completely.

Think globally

OUR WORLD

As the population in our world grows, so too will the pressure to log forests. Developed countries used to be covered with forests. The forests were chopped down for fuel and building materials, to clear land to build cities and farms, and to make mines to dig for raw materials. Now people living in countries with the remaining natural forests are beginning to cut them down too.

To protect the remaining forests, we need to manage them with thought and planning. The World Wildlife Fund, together with timber traders and shops, has begun an organization called the Forest Stewardship Council (FSC). The council gives a certificate to logging companies that cause as little damage as possible to the forests. The companies can then use the FSC label on their products. People who buy products made from wood can decide to buy from that company instead of the ones doing more damage.

▲ The FSC label has been stamped onto this timber.

STOP & THINK

Can we expect rainforest countries, most of them still developing, to make all the sacrifices needed to protect the remaining forests?

Governments in action

Rainforests benefit our whole world, so it is up to our whole world to help save them. Some governments and banks in developed countries are helping to pay off poorer countries' debts if they agree to protect the forests. This helps save large areas of forest that would otherwise have been logged to raise money to pay the debts.

In 1992 governments from around the world met at an Earth Summit in Brazil. It was the world's biggest meeting. All the leaders at the meeting signed an agreement called Agenda 21. It is a plan for using—and looking after—our world in the 21st century. All countries can do more to keep our world healthy. The strength of Agenda 21 is that the world's leaders agreed that we need to take action.

▲ These children were part of the Earth Summit in Brazil in 1992.

Agenda 21: Aims for our forests

- Prevent the destruction of forests.
- Replant as many trees as possible.
- Preserve forest habitats and prevent plants from becoming extinct.
- Show how to use and value forest products.
- Try to understand and share indigenous forest knowledge.
- Respect the rights of forest tribes to live in the forest.

YOU CAN DO iT!

- Write to politicians and tell them what you think needs to be done to protect forests.
- Talk to your parents about what you can do to help forests.
- Check if there are any national parks, reserves or tree planting groups in your area. Volunteer to help.

Sustaining our world

To survive on this planet, we need to take and use the things our world gives us. But we also need to keep all the parts of our world working in balance. Scientists call it ecologically sustainable development. It means taking only what we need from our world to live today, and at the same time keeping our world healthy so it can keep giving in the future.

We need to consider the needs of the timber industry, wildlife, people, and the future of our world when deciding how to manage forests. It is a hard balance to achieve. If we recognize the special value of natural forests, and use them carefully and for the right purposes, we can do it.

Everything in our world is connected. If we damage one part, we can affect the other parts. If we look after one part, we can help protect all the other parts. The future of our world depends on our actions now.

▼ The different parts of our world are all connected.

30

Glossary

acid a chemical that eats away solid material

atmosphere the thin layer of gases that surrounds Earth

biodiversity a mixture of a group of animals or plants

carbon dioxide a gas that animals breathe out and plants take in

climate the usual weather conditions in an area

consumed used up a product or resource

developed countries countries where the way of life is based on the use of resources by industries

developing countries countries based on farming that are trying to develop their resources

equator an imaginary line around the middle of the surface of Earth

evaporates changes from a liquid into a gas. For example, if you boil water (liquid) it changes into water vapor (gas)

global warming an increase in the temperature of Earth's climate, caused by the greenhouse effect

habitats the natural homes of plants or animals

hydroelectricity energy generated from the movement of water

indigenous originally living in an area

old-growth forest mostly undisturbed, natural forest

oxygen the gas in the air that all plants and animals need to live

plantation forests a large area of land where trees or crops are grown

raw materials materials used to make something else

renewable able to be used without reducing stocks or causing pollution

reservoir the lake that forms behind a dam

resources things that people make use of

species any group of living things that can breed together to produce offspring

Index